Jobs People Do

Teachers

by Mary Meinking

PEBBLE
a capstone imprint

Pebble Explore is published by Pebble, an imprint of Capstone.
1710 Roe Crest Drive
North Mankato, Minnesota 56003
www.capstonepub.com

Library of Congress Cataloging-in-Publication Data
Names: Meinking, Mary, author. | Pebble (Firm)
Title: Teachers / by Mary Meinking.
Other titles: Jobs people do.
Description: North Mankato, Minnesota : Pebble a Capstone imprint, 2020. | Series: Jobs people do | "Pebble Explore is published by Pebble, an imprint of Capstone"--T.p. verso. | Audience: Ages 6-8 years | Summary: "Teachers help students become excellent learners and wonderful adults. Readers will find out the different types of roles teachers have, the tools they use, and how people get this rewarding and difficult job"-- Provided by publisher.
Identifiers: LCCN 2019048284 (print) | LCCN 2019048285 (ebook) | ISBN 9781977113801 (Library Binding) | ISBN 9781977118158 (Paperback) | ISBN 9781977113887 (eBook PDF) Subjects: LCSH: Teachers--Juvenile literature. | Teaching--Vocational guidance--Juvenile literature. | Teacher-student relationships--Juvenile literature.
Classification: LCC LB1775 .M495 2020 (print) | LCC LB1775 (ebook) | DDC 371.1--dc23
LC record available at https://lccn.loc.gov/2019048284
LC ebook record available at https://lccn.loc.gov/2019048285

Image Credits
iStockphoto: gradyreese, 10, lisegagne, 12, manonallard, 21, Rawpixel, 26-27; Newscom: Fine Art Images/Album, 28; Shutterstock: Billion Photos, 19 (paper), Gorodenkoff, 24, Green Leaf, 19 (stapler, pencils), ifong, 19 (laptop), michaeljung, 15, Monkey Business Images, Cover, 5, 6, 7, 9, 11, 13, 16, 23, Popova Valeriya, 20, Syda Productions, 25, wavebreakmedia, 1, 17, YAKOBCHUK VIACHESLAV, 14

Editorial Credits
Editor: Gena Chester; Designer: Kyle Grenz; Media Researcher: Jo Miller; Production Specialist: Kathy McColley

Printed in the United States 6520

Table of Contents

Words in **bold** are in the glossary.

What Is a Teacher?

The first bell of the day rings. **Students** go to their desks. The teacher is ready to begin today's lesson.

Teachers help students every day. They explain things to their students. Good teachers make their students want to learn more.

pg 20+21
pg 18,19,20,21
pg 2,6,8

Teachers like being around children. Most work with certain ages. Some focus on only one subject. Others work with students who need extra help.

Teachers love their jobs. They must be **patient**. They make sure students follow the rules. They help young people learn.

What Teachers Do

Teachers help their students learn. They give lessons about new facts and ideas. They write **quizzes** and tests. They give quizzes and tests to students. Sometimes students give wrong answers on a test. Teachers help them know why they were wrong.

Teachers for lower **grades** teach basic skills to their students. They teach reading, writing, math, and science. They use games and activities to help young students with new skills.

Some teachers take their students on field trips. They ride buses. They go to **museums**, parks, or other spots.

A teacher and her class on a field trip

Middle grade teachers cover one or two subjects. One teacher might teach subjects like math or science. One could teach English.

Upper grade teachers cover one subject. Some are English, science, or math teachers. They may teach special subjects such as life science or painting.

A teacher grading papers

Teachers help students get ready for **college**. They teach students to think on their own. They give out more work, quizzes, and tests. The older the students are, the harder the work.

How Teachers Help

Teachers help students learn. But they also help students become better people. They show students how to work with others. They help shape a student's life.

Teachers set **goals** for their students. This means students have something to work toward. Teachers want students to get better.

People learn in different ways. Teachers change the way they teach to fit their students. Some students learn better by listening. Some learn by watching videos. Others learn by doing projects.

Some students have a hard time learning. Teachers can give extra help. They may meet with parents. Some teachers **tutor** students. Teachers want all of their students to succeed.

Teachers' Clothes and Tools

Teachers must dress in nice clothes. They can't wear ripped or sloppy clothes.

Most teachers stand during class. They need to wear comfy shoes. Teachers walk a lot in the school and outside. They don't want shoes to hurt their feet.

Gym teachers wear exercise clothes. They work out with students.

Most teachers have **supplies** in the classroom. Some supplies are for the teacher. Other supplies are for the students. Most teachers have a stapler, pencils, paper, and other things on their desks.

Many young students work on their own whiteboard. Older students work on a computer.

Many teachers use a computer to give lessons or show videos. They also use large whiteboards on the wall. They write lessons or notes on the boards.

Teacher Tools

pencils

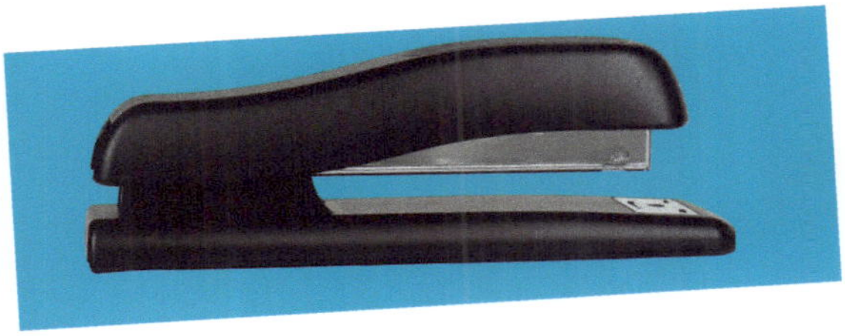

stapler

laptop

paper

Where Teachers Work

Most teachers work in public schools. About one in seven teachers work in private schools. Teachers work at many grade levels. They also teach at **preschools** and **kindergartens**.

Teacher's jobs aren't over when the last bell rings. They grade papers and tests after school. Teachers get ready for what they are going to teach the next day. After school hours, some teachers lead clubs. Some teachers **coach** sport teams.

Most schools run nine or ten months in a year. Teachers have summers off from teaching duties. Some teach summer school. Other teachers work at another job in summer.

How to Become a Teacher

Do you want to become a public school teacher? Teachers need at least four years of college. In college, they learn how best to teach, plan lessons, and write tests.

In their last year of college, they student teach. They watch and learn from other teachers. Then it's their turn to teach the class.

After college, they need to take a state test. They also are tested on the subject they will be teaching.

Teachers keep learning. Every year they must take classes to learn new skills.

Some teachers go back to college. Or they take extra classes to teach college students. College teachers can make more money.

Teachers taking a college class

Famous Teachers

In 1887, Anne Sullivan became the teacher of Helen Keller, a girl who was blind and deaf. Sullivan was also blind. She helped Helen graduate from college.

Maria Montessori was the only girl in her school. In 1907, she opened a school in Rome. At the school children taught themselves. Today, Montessori schools let children learn in their own way.

Anne Sullivan

Fast Facts

- **What Teachers Do:**
  Teachers help educate young people.

- **Key Tools:**
  pencils, paper, computer, whiteboard

- **Key Clothes:**
  comfy shoes and professional clothing

- **Education Needed:**
  Four years of college

- **Key Function:**
  teach children

- **Famous Teachers:**
  Anne Sullivan and Maria Montessori

Glossary

coach (KOHCH)—a person who trains a sports team

college (KAH-lug)—a school that students go to after high school

goal (GOHL)—something that you aim for or work toward

grade (GRAYD)—a level in school

kindergarten (KIN-dur-GAR-din)—a school or class children go to before first grade

museum (mew-ZEE-uhm)—a place where objects of art, history, or science are shown

patient (PAY-shunt)—calm during difficult times

preschool (pre-SKOOL)—a starting school before a child is old enough for kindergarten or grade school

quiz (KWIZ)—a short test of knowledge

student (STOO-duhnt)—a person who goes to a school to learn

supplies (suh-PLYS)—things needed to do something

tutor (TOO-tur)—a teacher who gives lessons to just one student or a small group of students

Read More

Heos, Bridget. *Let's Meet a Teacher*. Minneapolis, MN: Millbrook Press, 2013.

Liebman, Daniel. *I Want to Be a Teacher*. Richmond Hills, OT, Canada: Firefly Books, 2018.

Meister, Cari. *Teachers*. Minneapolis, MN: Jump, 2016.

Internet Sites

How to Become a Teacher
https://www.learnhowtobecome.org/teacher/

Career Quiz
https://www.kidzworld.com/quiz/203

Meet the Teacher Video
https://www.youtube.com/watch?v=sYgKx1zOY3Q

Index